This is the TEA TASTING JOURNAL
of:

....

If found, please contact me at:

....
....
....
....
....

Thank you!

ChaDao

Dedicated to all sentient beings that bring happiness to others through the joy of tea.

TEA

TASTING

JOURNAL

A diary for
your adventures in tea

ChaDao UK

Introduction and foreword by

Venerable Lama Tenzin (Tony) Malone

ISBN-13: **978-1535103602**

SKU: 2-1-3

Printed using an environmentally considered process on recycled paper and cover board.

In producing this Tea Journal we would like to thank the following for their support and encouragement in all things tea: The Scouts, David Wraight, Ciaran Buesnel, The Late Venerable GrandMaster Lama Tai-Yun Gyatso, Troll, Dawn, Andy, Cat and Vic from the World Buddhist Scout Council, Banjo the cat and Teacup the dog.

This publication is dedicated to the Explorer Scouts of the 38th and 40th Strood Sea Scout Unit, whom have tried so many teas in so many ways and in so many places with myself and other leaders in our TeaTravels.

ChaDao UK

Visit our website to learn more about the world of tea.

ChaDao.co.uk

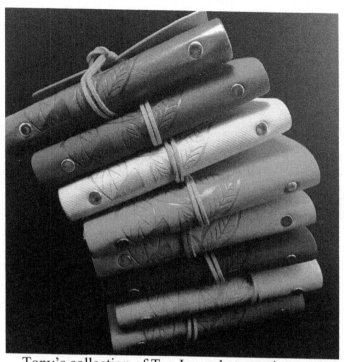

Tony's collection of Tea Journals, spanning over twenty-five years of tea notes and tastings.

Introduction

Dear Tea Friends,

I am so very thankful for so many responses to the first edition of this book from all over the world! For over twenty-five years I have travelled with a small bound notebook studying both tea flavours and noting 'The Ways of Tea' from around the world! These notes both serve as a professional reference in my work as a Tea Master and also as a personal diary. I fondly look back through these journals remembering, cups of tea on steam trains, hiking with friends while making tea in some far-flung forest or mountain, or simply a family moment brought together with the creation of a new tea blend.

In this Tea Journal, I have attempted to compile a page layout for you to fill in as you experience tea. I hope this guide will help and develop your tea knowledge, your senses of taste and aroma, and to also encourage you to explore new teas from all over the world.

In my own tea journals, I have added small sketches, watercolours, 'tea' paintings or stapled in photographs. I recommend you to do the same and shape this journal, and future journals into your own personal experience.

Remember that tea is always best shared. So please do upload photos of your journals to the internet when you feel like sharing these tea discoveries! -And tag us in them as we love hearing about other people's joy in tea!

No tea diary should ever be simply an index or reference guide; it is a celebration of your journey in life with tea!

Most of all, embrace 'The Way of Tea', be kind, show compassion and engage in mindfulness in all that you do and join us all on the great voyage of tea.

Wishing you love, laughter and good tea in life.

Venerable Lama Tenzin (Tony) Malone
Master of Tea, ChaDao Lama, GongFu Teacher.

The Art Of Tea Tasting

A page and notes on flavours from one of Tony's
Journals. -note the ceramic Cha He used to examine
the leaves before infusion in the Gong Fu Style.

Tea tasting is an art form that was first documented by the 'Father of Tea', LuYu in approximately 760 CE during the Tang Dynasty in China. LuYu pioneered not only a higher appreciation of tea and its flavour but also the of recording and note taking of the complexities of tea culture.

Today, tea tasting is achieved for three main reasons; a record to keep an accurate taste in a particular tea blend over many years; for recording and discovering new teas and new plantations; to keep a diary of one's Tea-Travels and life through tea.

When tasting teas it is important to note the following main areas:

Origin - Elevation - Colour - Aroma – Taste

Aroma and taste will be linked, but also different. Try to think of similar smells and flavours to link your notes to. Is it sweet or sour? Fresh and crisp or 'musty' and 'ancient'? Does it improve over second or third or even fourth infusions? How does it make you feel?

There are many ways of experiencing tea. The next few pages is an introduction to two tea drinking techniques used in tea tasting. It doesn't matter how you taste tea yourself as long as you enjoy it!

A tea tasting bowl and cup as used in 'commercial' or Western Style Tea Tasting.

Western or commercial style tea tasting

This more industrial style involves three main pieces of equipment:

> A silver tea tasting spoon
> A white china tea bowl
> A Toothed Gai-Wan style Teapot with a

handle

This technique is about observing the colour and sampling a small batch of the tea. One adds the tea to the pot with boiling water, allow to infuse then empty the contents through the cup's teeth into the white bowl. The leaves will then be tipped onto the lid of the teapot/cup for inspection.

The tea taster then observes the colour and aroma from the white bowl and then using his or her personal tea tasting spoon take a sample to taste by 'slurping'. On days with lots of tastings the custom is to spit the tea out into a container.

This technique allows a good efficient taste of a new tea or to work on the consistency of maintaining a particular tea blend to avoid any deviance from the blend recipe. We use this technique ourselves for blending tea by hand.

Gong Fu style Tea Tasting.

Gong Fu Cha style tea tasting

Perhaps the original, and most enjoyable, way to professionally taste tea is the Gong Fu Cha (or Kung Fu) tea ceremony. This meditative way of making tea has inspired many other tea ceremonies around the world. It originated in North Tibet regions and spread north into China and south into Nepal and India.

The basic equipment normally used is:
> A Tea tray with waste water compartment
> Yixing clay (Tea clay) small tea pot
> A tea jug
> A tea strainer and a Cha He (tea presenter)
> Small tea bowls

It consists of brewing the tea infusions in a small yixing tea clay small teapot. Pouring the tea into a glass or ceramic jug to observe the colour, and then pouring the tea into the small tea bowls to be drunk. Making tea in this way can become both an art form and a meditation due to the highly skilled nature of the tea master's performance.

We use this method a lot to test teas over various infusions and also to enjoy tea socially with friends, discussing tea and life over many little cups.
The Gong Fu Ceremony is very adaptable for any setting, mood, culture and personal expressions.

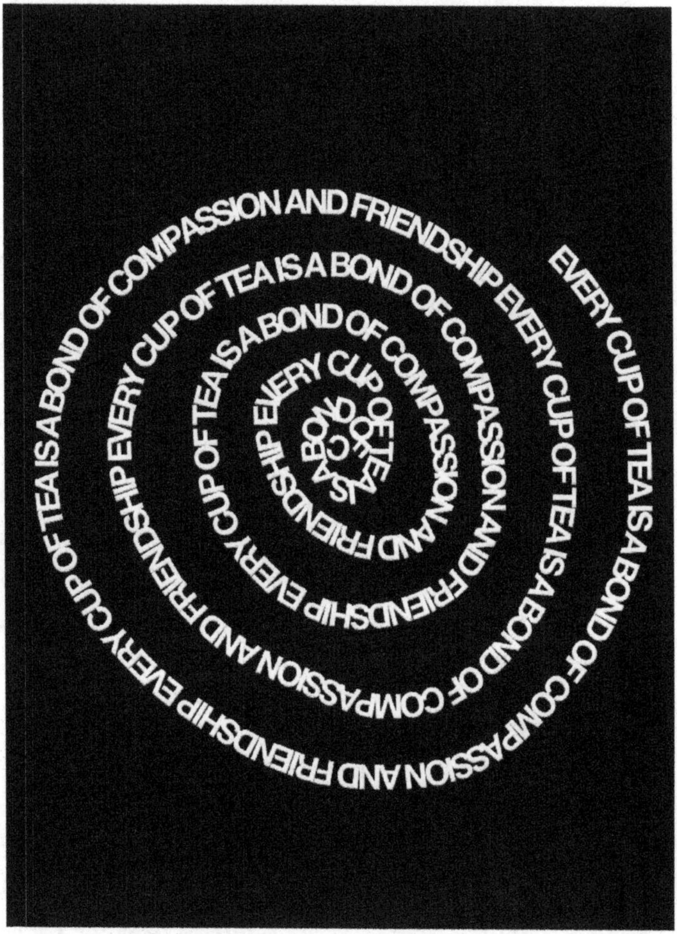

The Way Of Tea
(Cha Dao)

"Each and every cup of tea is a universal bond of friendship and compassion."

The guiding principle of my work in the ways of tea, or ChaDao, as it is also known is that by sharing a simple experiences friendships and compassion can be generated and shared.

We all know tea can be made and enjoyed in many hundreds of ways. A family shared moment, a refreshing point of enjoyment during the day or as part of a stylised ritual or meditation. Its possibilities are endless. You can even drink tea simply because it is there.

ChaDao or 'The Way of Tea' comes from the Chinese Daoism way of describing the wonder in all things. It is perhaps through the Zen Buddhism (ChaDou) practice of Japan that the world has learned most of these curious tea ceremonies, rituals and meditations.

Ever since the intertwined histories of tea and the faiths of the east came together tea has become a world of special meanings. Faiths such as Taoism, the various forms of Buddhism and Hinduism have all celebrated how tea can aid meditation practice together with is unique way of bringing a community together.

The 'Sage of Tea' himself, LuYu first explored the making and brewing of tea as an skilled form of mindfulness. By Mindfulness we mean a state by which you can temporarily loose a sense of self in concentration, noticing nothing except the intricate details of the act you are performing.

Teaism in its purest sense is the finding or seeking of enlightenment and peace in the everyday world around us.

Tea was once described to me by my teacher, a Tibetan Lama as "A dance between life and the elements", an exploration of presence and community, connecting everything through space and time." It is a beautiful analogy of how you could come to understand the role of tea as a global link across humanity.

My view of Teaism is to accept it as the act of appreciating the way a simple thing such as tea can create infusions of understanding and compassion. This aspect travels across all faiths, continents and communities as an empowering force for good.

Throughout my years of study of tea and Buddhism, I have learned most, not from study, but by sharing. By teaching I have learned new ways of seeing from my students, everyone is your teacher.

Over the next few pages I have outlined a simple tea meditation which I encourage you to try. It doesn't require much concentration, it doesn't require any particular faith study, it simply requires a sense of wonder and thankfulness.

In Buddhism, we have the concept of Bodhicitta; a spontaneous wish to attain enlightenment motivated by great compassion for all sentient beings, accompanied by a falling away of the attachment to the illusion of a sense of self as separate from the world. This similar concept appears in almost every other faith or no faith in some way, it is a point of purity and good.

I hope in someway everyone experiences this, with or without tea, and learns how to teach ways to bring people together in friendship and compassion.

Tenzin (Tony), Teaching tea and Buddhism to young
Cub Scouts in London, 2018

A Simple Tea Meditation

This is a simple 10 minute or one hour, as you require meditation. Its aim is to simply take a moment out of your day to sit in a present moment of mindfulness.

It's aim is to cultivate a sense of reverence for all life. Reduce stress and anxiety which helps you find a greater clarity of mind and improved concentration.

It's a simple starting point for other seated meditations and mindfulness training. Simply by consistently applying this meditation over a month will actively help to bring about a greater sense of understanding of your own mind.

Each of the following steps focus fully on the task at hand, make each step your sole point of effort and mental focuses. Allow your mind to totally appreciate all aspects of the tasks.

Step 1, Make your tea.

Any tea, doesn't matter what or how. Notice the boiling of the water, the steam, the infusion of colour into water.

When your tea is made simply "sit with your tea" notice the aroma, the colour, the interaction of steam and air. Consider the process that the tea has took to change. From seed to plant to package to cup. Consider all the human effort and development for you to simply sit now in the present with your tea.

Step 2, Give Thanks

Be thankful to all those who have had a hand in producing your tea, their efforts. Then consider the people and effort to bring you water to drink and electric or gas to heat and boil that water.

Consider how easy it is to take this act of 'simply sitting with tea' for granted when others do not have tea, drinking water or heat...

Appreciate the cup of tea and everything that had to happen, that thought to yourself and the knowledge that you also depend on infinite living and non-living things to exist as you are now in this moment just as the tea does.

Step 3, Drinking your tea.

Now the important part, you have prepared your tea, you have been thankful and respected those who have expanded effort to bring this tea to you.

Take a sip at a time and notice the aroma, the taste of every sip.

Between sips focus on your breathing and then sip again.

If your mind wanders off (as is natural) notice where it takes you and then bring it back to your tea and the task at hand.

Be fully focused for the drinking of your tea, understand that this moment and this cup of tea will never exist again. It is an example in impermanence. A magical point that can never repeat.

Step 4, Giving thanks again.

As you bring your meditation to a close, give thanks once again, considering and congratulating all those who helped bring this tea to this point in time with you.

Now you're finished it is important to understand the ritual of this, a simple Tea Meditation such as this is an example of how you can find the divine enlightenment in most of the activities of your everyday life. Notice throughout your day how positively transformative this approach to the everyday can be.

Teenagers learning about ChaDao, and Tea at the Gilwell Buddha Sala, 2018

Tea Leaf Grading Terms
And Other Notes

The Five Tea Types:

White Tea
Fresh or freshly wilted tea in an un-oxidised state.

Yellow Tea
Un-wilted and un-oxidised, allowed to yellow naturally in little or no sunlight.

Green Tea
Un-wilted and un-oxidised tea.

Oolong Tea
Wilted, bruised and part oxidised tea.

Black Tea
(Sometimes known as Red Tea in China) Wilted, bruised, fully oxidised, and sometimes crushed.

Extra terms we use for easier note taking:

Post-Fermented Green Tea
Green tea allowed to ferment. (Black Tea in China)

Needles
Very Young tender stems of new plant growth. Can be white, green or yellow tea type.

PuErh
Compressed Tea, formed into a shape and aged.

Tisanes / Infusions
Fruit or Hebal infusions that contain no tea or other plant matter from the Camellia Sinensis plant.

Leaf Processing Types

Orthodox
Whole leaf or Broken leaf made using traditional methods.

CTC
Machine ground to form a uniform particle of tea. Invented by William McKercher in 1930 to replace the final stages of Orthodox production in lower grade teas.

Milk, Sugar, Honey etc.

It is a common myth that good quality tea should not have milk or sugar added. In fact some teas are greatly improved by these additions. It is always worth reading the packet or consulting any available 'Taster's notes' such as found in our own teas to experiment further with these.

The Camellia Sinensis:

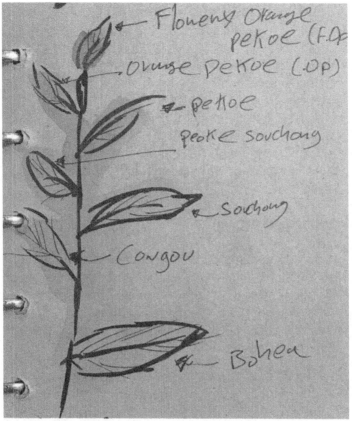

Flowery Orange Pekoe (F.O

Orange Pekoe (OP)

Pekoe

Peoke Souchong

Souchong

Congou

Bohea

Some of the leaf grades an categories relate directly
to where on a tea plant the have been picked from.

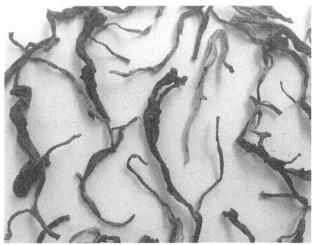

Above: Withered and hand rolled whole tea leaves.
Below: Japanese Sencha steamed green tea leaves

Generic Terms and Abbreviations

Choppy – Leaves of various sizes.
Fannings – 'Tea Dust' or CTC Particles such as found in Tea bags.
Flowery – 2nd or 3rd Flush loose leaves with tips.
Golden Flowery – Early Season young tips and buds.
Tippy – Lots of plant tips.
Flush – A tea plant harvest.
Musctl. – Muscatel
OP. – Orange Peoke
Cl. – Clonal
Ch. – China
Qu. – Queen Jat
FP. – Flowery Peoke
PS. – Peoke Souchong
S. – Souchong
…Ex.Spl. – Extra Special Tea.

Whole Leaf Grades

OP1
Slightly delicate, long, wire like leaf.

OPA
Bold, long leaf with tight or open binding/rolling.

OP (Orange Peoke)
Main grade of quality tea, OP.1 and OP no tips.

OP.superior
OP grade but from Indonesia.

F.OP (Flowery.OP)
Best quality tea with a long leaf. Usually known as 1st
Grade in China or 2nd In Assam and Bangladesh.

F.OP1
An F.OP of higher quality.

G.F.OP1 (Golden F.OP1)
Uncommon in Darjeeling and Assam. An F.OP1 with
more young tips and buds.

T.G.F.OP (Tippy Golden F.OP)
Top section of tips, main tea grade for Darjeeling or
Assam.
T.G.F.OP1
The highest grade of tea normally available in
Darjeeling or Assam. Excellent leaves.

S.F.T.G.F.OP1 (Special Flower T.G.F.OP1)
The finest possible grade T.G.F.OP1 tea usually

possible, all hand picked, hand sorted and hand processed. Normally at least 1 quarter tips per batch.

F.T.G.F.O.P(1)
A very rare Darjeeling grade of the best possible tea.

F.T.G.F.O.P1.ExSpl.
A once every few hundred years finest grade of tea.

Broken Leaf Grades

BT
Broken Tea: Black, open fleshy leaves, can be quit bulky. Southern India, Sri Lanka, Sumatra examples of BT tea are the most common.

BP
Most common Broken Peoke grade in all tea regions. (BP not usually a Darjeeling grade)

BP.S (BP.Souchong)
A common BP grade and term in Assam and Darjeeling tea regions.

FP (Flowery Peoke)
Higher quality broken leaf grade from South India, Kenya and Sri Lanka. Coarser, fleshier leaves.

BOP
Main broken tea grade in Assam, South India, Java, China and Japan.

F.BOP (Flowery BOP)
Flowery BOP coarse leaves with some tips. Common in Assam, Sri Lanka, Indonesia, China and Bangladesh. In the Americas this grade is coarser and blacker.
F.BOP.F
Finest grade F.BOP usually from lower level plantations in Sri Lanka.

G.F.BOP (sometimes G.F.BOP1)
Second grade tea, un even leaves and some tips with

the (1) denoting a better quality. Often used in blending.

T.G.F.BOP1
Highest quality broken leaves, with a noticeably higher proportion of tips. Best broken grade is usually from Assam closely followed by Darjeeling.

Fannings Grades (ie. Teabags)

PF
Peoke Fannings

OF
Orange Fannings, usually used in North India, Africa or
South America.

FOF
Flowery Orange Fannings. Common in Assam, Bangladesh, Argentina.

GFOF
Golden FOF normally only used in Darjeeling tea bags.

TGFOF
Tippy GFOF

BOPF
Main grade of black leaf tea with or without added ingredients. Uniform particle size. Usually no tips.

Dust Grades (ie. Matcha)

D1
Dust 1, from Sri Lanka, Indonesia, China, Japan, Africa and Americas.

PD
Peoke dust. (PD1 is an Indonesia only grade)

RD
Red Peoke dust.

FD
Fine dust.

GD
Golden dust.

SRD
Super red dust.

SFD
Super fine dust.

PM
Pestle and Mortar ground dust.

CTC
Machine processed dust.

LuYu, The Sage of Tea waiting for an infusion.

Your own
Tea Tasting Journal
Notes

Tea name: **Orange Blossom Oolong**

SAMPLE PAGE TO GIVE YOU SOME IDEAS

Tea Date: **1 June '16** Current location: **London, UK**

Brand/Supplier: **Deeper Understanding of Tea**

Leaf type: **F.G.OP1**

Origin plantation or growing region: **Meipei Mountain farm, just outside of Taipei, Taiwan**

Elevation grown: **3500-4000ft**

Ethical notes: **Family farm** Environmental notes: **Organic**

Number of infusions: **3**

Intensity: Light -------X-- Full Bodied

Colour: **Dark Green,** (spill some in the box here to stain the paper)

Aroma: **Heavy on Orange flowers, hint of grass freshness.**

Tasting notes: **A wonderful tea, really crisp. Refreshing flowery taste with strong hints of citrus.**

Other notes on this tea:

Currently sitting in my favourite café in London with friends while trying this tea. It has just stopped raining!

The tea is wonderful, really quite special. The firs infusion is perhaps the lesser one. Second infusion was improved but the third mellowed the tea enough to allow the Oolong characteristics to come through stronger

A quick sketch of the view from the window of the café here.

Tea name:

Tea Date: Current location:

Brand/Supplier:

Leaf type:

Origin plantation or growing region:

Elevation grown:

Ethical notes: Environmental notes:

Number of infusions:

Intensity: Light ---------- Full Bodied

Colour:

Aroma:

Tasting notes:

Other notes on this tea:

Tea name:

Tea Date: Current location:

Brand/Supplier:

Leaf type:

Origin plantation or growing region:

Elevation grown:

Ethical notes: Environmental notes:

Number of infusions:

Intensity: Light ---------- Full Bodied

Colour:

Aroma:

Tasting notes:

Other notes on this tea:

Tea name:

Tea Date: Current location:

Brand/Supplier:

Leaf type:

Origin plantation or growing region:

Elevation grown:

Ethical notes: Environmental notes:

Number of infusions:

Intensity: Light ---------- Full Bodied

Colour:

Aroma:

Tasting notes:

Other notes on this tea:

Tea name:

Tea Date: Current location:

Brand/Supplier:

Leaf type:

Origin plantation or growing region:

Elevation grown:

Ethical notes: Environmental notes:

Number of infusions:

Intensity: Light ---------- Full Bodied

Colour:

Aroma:

Tasting notes:

Other notes on this tea:

Tea name:

Tea Date: Current location:

Brand/Supplier:

Leaf type:

Origin plantation or growing region:

Elevation grown:

Ethical notes: Environmental notes:

Number of infusions:

Intensity: Light ---------- Full Bodied

Colour:

Aroma:

Tasting notes:

Other notes on this tea:

Tea name:

Tea Date: Current location:

Brand/Supplier:

Leaf type:

Origin plantation or growing region:

Elevation grown:

Ethical notes: Environmental notes:

Number of infusions:

Intensity: Light ---------- Full Bodied

Colour:

Aroma:

Tasting notes:

Other notes on this tea:

Tea name:

Tea Date: Current location:

Brand/Supplier:

Leaf type:

Origin plantation or growing region:

Elevation grown:

Ethical notes: Environmental notes:

Number of infusions:

Intensity: Light ---------- Full Bodied

Colour:

Aroma:

Tasting notes:

Other notes on this tea:

Tea name:

Tea Date: Current location:

Brand/Supplier:

Leaf type:

Origin plantation or growing region:

Elevation grown:

Ethical notes: Environmental notes:

Number of infusions:

Intensity: Light ---------- Full Bodied

Colour:

Aroma:

Tasting notes:

Other notes on this tea:

Tea name:

Tea Date: Current location:

Brand/Supplier:

Leaf type:

Origin plantation or growing region:

Elevation grown:

Ethical notes: Environmental notes:

Number of infusions:

Intensity: Light ---------- Full Bodied

Colour:

Aroma:

Tasting notes:

Other notes on this tea:

Tea name:

Tea Date: Current location:

Brand/Supplier:

Leaf type:

Origin plantation or growing region:

Elevation grown:

Ethical notes: Environmental notes:

Number of infusions:

Intensity: Light ---------- Full Bodied

Colour:

Aroma:

Tasting notes:

Other notes on this tea:

Tea name:

Tea Date: Current location:

Brand/Supplier:

Leaf type:

Origin plantation or growing region:

Elevation grown:

Ethical notes: Environmental notes:

Number of infusions:

Intensity: Light ---------- Full Bodied

Colour:

Aroma:

Tasting notes:

Other notes on this tea:

Tea name:

Tea Date: Current location:

Brand/Supplier:

Leaf type:

Origin plantation or growing region:

Elevation grown:

Ethical notes: Environmental notes:

Number of infusions:

Intensity: Light ---------- Full Bodied

Colour:

Aroma:

Tasting notes:

Other notes on this tea:

Tea name:

Tea Date: Current location:

Brand/Supplier:

Leaf type:

Origin plantation or growing region:

Elevation grown:

Ethical notes: Environmental notes:

Number of infusions:

Intensity: Light ---------- Full Bodied

Colour:

Aroma:

Tasting notes:

Other notes on this tea:

Tea name:

Tea Date: Current location:

Brand/Supplier:

Leaf type:

Origin plantation or growing region:

Elevation grown:

Ethical notes: Environmental notes:

Number of infusions:

Intensity: Light ---------- Full Bodied

Colour:

Aroma:

Tasting notes:

Other notes on this tea:

Tea name:

Tea Date: Current location:

Brand/Supplier:

Leaf type:

Origin plantation or growing region:

Elevation grown:

Ethical notes: Environmental notes:

Number of infusions:

Intensity: Light ---------- Full Bodied

Colour:

Aroma:

Tasting notes:

Other notes on this tea:

Tea name:

Tea Date: Current location:

Brand/Supplier:

Leaf type:

Origin plantation or growing region:

Elevation grown:

Ethical notes: Environmental notes:

Number of infusions:

Intensity: Light ---------- Full Bodied

Colour:

Aroma:

Tasting notes:

Other notes on this tea:

Tea name:

Tea Date: Current location:

Brand/Supplier:

Leaf type:

Origin plantation or growing region:

Elevation grown:

Ethical notes: Environmental notes:

Number of infusions:

Intensity: Light ---------- Full Bodied

Colour:

Aroma:

Tasting notes:

Other notes on this tea:

Tea name:

Tea Date: Current location:

Brand/Supplier:

Leaf type:

Origin plantation or growing region:

Elevation grown:

Ethical notes: Environmental notes:

Number of infusions:

Intensity: Light ---------- Full Bodied

Colour:

Aroma:

Tasting notes:

Other notes on this tea:

Tea name:

Tea Date: Current location:

Brand/Supplier:

Leaf type:

Origin plantation or growing region:

Elevation grown:

Ethical notes: Environmental notes:

Number of infusions:

Intensity: Light ---------- Full Bodied

Colour:

Aroma:

Tasting notes:

Other notes on this tea:

Tea name:

Tea Date: Current location:

Brand/Supplier:

Leaf type:

Origin plantation or growing region:

Elevation grown:

Ethical notes: Environmental notes:

Number of infusions:

Intensity: Light ---------- Full Bodied

Colour:

Aroma:

Tasting notes:

Other notes on this tea:

Tea name:

Tea Date: Current location:

Brand/Supplier:

Leaf type:

Origin plantation or growing region:

Elevation grown:

Ethical notes: Environmental notes:

Number of infusions:

Intensity: Light ---------- Full Bodied

Colour:

Aroma:

Tasting notes:

Other notes on this tea:

Tea name:

Tea Date: Current location:

Brand/Supplier:

Leaf type:

Origin plantation or growing region:

Elevation grown:

Ethical notes: Environmental notes:

Number of infusions:

Intensity: Light ---------- Full Bodied

Colour:

Aroma:

Tasting notes:

Other notes on this tea:

Tea name:

Tea Date: Current location:

Brand/Supplier:

Leaf type:

Origin plantation or growing region:

Elevation grown:

Ethical notes: Environmental notes:

Number of infusions:

Intensity: Light ---------- Full Bodied

Colour:

Aroma:

Tasting notes:

Other notes on this tea:

Tea name:

Tea Date: Current location:

Brand/Supplier:

Leaf type:

Origin plantation or growing region:

Elevation grown:

Ethical notes: Environmental notes:

Number of infusions:

Intensity: Light ---------- Full Bodied

Colour:

Aroma:

Tasting notes:

Other notes on this tea:

Tea name:

Tea Date: Current location:

Brand/Supplier:

Leaf type:

Origin plantation or growing region:

Elevation grown:

Ethical notes: Environmental notes:

Number of infusions:

Intensity: Light ---------- Full Bodied

Colour:

Aroma:

Tasting notes:

Other notes on this tea:

Tea name:

Tea Date: Current location:

Brand/Supplier:

Leaf type:

Origin plantation or growing region:

Elevation grown:

Ethical notes: Environmental notes:

Number of infusions:

Intensity: Light ---------- Full Bodied

Colour:

Aroma:

Tasting notes:

Other notes on this tea:

Tea name:

Tea Date: Current location:

Brand/Supplier:

Leaf type:

Origin plantation or growing region:

Elevation grown:

Ethical notes: Environmental notes:

Number of infusions:

Intensity: Light ---------- Full Bodied

Colour:

Aroma:

Tasting notes:

Other notes on this tea:

Tea name:

Tea Date: Current location:

Brand/Supplier:

Leaf type:

Origin plantation or growing region:

Elevation grown:

Ethical notes: Environmental notes:

Number of infusions:

Intensity: Light ---------- Full Bodied

Colour:

Aroma:

Tasting notes:

Other notes on this tea:

Tea name:

Tea Date: Current location:

Brand/Supplier:

Leaf type:

Origin plantation or growing region:

Elevation grown:

Ethical notes: Environmental notes:

Number of infusions:

Intensity: Light ---------- Full Bodied

Colour:

Aroma:

Tasting notes:

Other notes on this tea:

Tea name:

Tea Date: Current location:

Brand/Supplier:

Leaf type:

Origin plantation or growing region:

Elevation grown:

Ethical notes: Environmental notes:

Number of infusions:

Intensity: Light ---------- Full Bodied

Colour:

Aroma:

Tasting notes:

Other notes on this tea:

Tea name:

Tea Date: Current location:

Brand/Supplier:

Leaf type:

Origin plantation or growing region:

Elevation grown:

Ethical notes: Environmental notes:

Number of infusions:

Intensity: Light ---------- Full Bodied

Colour:

Aroma:

Tasting notes:

Other notes on this tea:

Tea name:

Tea Date: Current location:

Brand/Supplier:

Leaf type:

Origin plantation or growing region:

Elevation grown:

Ethical notes: Environmental notes:

Number of infusions:

Intensity: Light ---------- Full Bodied

Colour:

Aroma:

Tasting notes:

Other notes on this tea:

Tea name:

Tea Date: Current location:

Brand/Supplier:

Leaf type:

Origin plantation or growing region:

Elevation grown:

Ethical notes: Environmental notes:

Number of infusions:

Intensity: Light ---------- Full Bodied

Colour:

Aroma:

Tasting notes:

Other notes on this tea:

Tea name:

Tea Date: Current location:

Brand/Supplier:

Leaf type:

Origin plantation or growing region:

Elevation grown:

Ethical notes: Environmental notes:

Number of infusions:

Intensity: Light ---------- Full Bodied

Colour:

Aroma:

Tasting notes:

Other notes on this tea:

Tea name:

Tea Date: Current location:

Brand/Supplier:

Leaf type:

Origin plantation or growing region:

Elevation grown:

Ethical notes: Environmental notes:

Number of infusions:

Intensity: Light ---------- Full Bodied

Colour:

Aroma:

Tasting notes:

Other notes on this tea:

Tea name:

Tea Date: Current location:

Brand/Supplier:

Leaf type:

Origin plantation or growing region:

Elevation grown:

Ethical notes: Environmental notes:

Number of infusions:

Intensity: Light ---------- Full Bodied

Colour:

Aroma:

Tasting notes:

Other notes on this tea:

Tea name:

Tea Date: Current location:

Brand/Supplier:

Leaf type:

Origin plantation or growing region:

Elevation grown:

Ethical notes: Environmental notes:

Number of infusions:

Intensity: Light ---------- Full Bodied

Colour:

Aroma:

Tasting notes:

Other notes on this tea:

Tea name:

Tea Date: Current location:

Brand/Supplier:

Leaf type:

Origin plantation or growing region:

Elevation grown:

Ethical notes: Environmental notes:

Number of infusions:

Intensity: Light ---------- Full Bodied

Colour:

Aroma:

Tasting notes:

Other notes on this tea:

Tea name:

Tea Date: Current location:

Brand/Supplier:

Leaf type:

Origin plantation or growing region:

Elevation grown:

Ethical notes: Environmental notes:

Number of infusions:

Intensity: Light ---------- Full Bodied

Colour:

Aroma:

Tasting notes:

Other notes on this tea:

Tea name:

Tea Date: Current location:

Brand/Supplier:

Leaf type:

Origin plantation or growing region:

Elevation grown:

Ethical notes: Environmental notes:

Number of infusions:

Intensity: Light ---------- Full Bodied

Colour:

Aroma:

Tasting notes:

Other notes on this tea:

Tea name:

Tea Date: Current location:

Brand/Supplier:

Leaf type:

Origin plantation or growing region:

Elevation grown:

Ethical notes: Environmental notes:

Number of infusions:

Intensity: Light ---------- Full Bodied

Colour:

Aroma:

Tasting notes:

Other notes on this tea:

Tea name:

Tea Date: Current location:

Brand/Supplier:

Leaf type:

Origin plantation or growing region:

Elevation grown:

Ethical notes: Environmental notes:

Number of infusions:

Intensity: Light ---------- Full Bodied

Colour:

Aroma:

Tasting notes:

Other notes on this tea:

Tea name:

Tea Date: Current location:

Brand/Supplier:

Leaf type:

Origin plantation or growing region:

Elevation grown:

Ethical notes: Environmental notes:

Number of infusions:

Intensity: Light ---------- Full Bodied

Colour:

Aroma:

Tasting notes:

Other notes on this tea:

Tea name:

Tea Date: Current location:

Brand/Supplier:

Leaf type:

Origin plantation or growing region:

Elevation grown:

Ethical notes: Environmental notes:

Number of infusions:

Intensity: Light ---------- Full Bodied

Colour:

Aroma:

Tasting notes:

Other notes on this tea:

Tea name:

Tea Date: Current location:

Brand/Supplier:

Leaf type:

Origin plantation or growing region:

Elevation grown:

Ethical notes: Environmental notes:

Number of infusions:

Intensity: Light ---------- Full Bodied

Colour:

Aroma:

Tasting notes:

Other notes on this tea:

Tea name:

Tea Date: Current location:

Brand/Supplier:

Leaf type:

Origin plantation or growing region:

Elevation grown:

Ethical notes: Environmental notes:

Number of infusions:

Intensity: Light ---------- Full Bodied

Colour:

Aroma:

Tasting notes:

Other notes on this tea:

Tea name:

Tea Date: Current location:

Brand/Supplier:

Leaf type:

Origin plantation or growing region:

Elevation grown:

Ethical notes: Environmental notes:

Number of infusions:

Intensity: Light ---------- Full Bodied

Colour:

Aroma:

Tasting notes:

Other notes on this tea:

Tea name:

Tea Date: Current location:

Brand/Supplier:

Leaf type:

Origin plantation or growing region:

Elevation grown:

Ethical notes: Environmental notes:

Number of infusions:

Intensity: Light ---------- Full Bodied

Colour:

Aroma:

Tasting notes:

Other notes on this tea:

Tea name:

Tea Date: Current location:

Brand/Supplier:

Leaf type:

Origin plantation or growing region:

Elevation grown:

Ethical notes: Environmental notes:

Number of infusions:

Intensity: Light ---------- Full Bodied

Colour:

Aroma:

Tasting notes:

Other notes on this tea:

Tea name:

Tea Date: Current location:

Brand/Supplier:

Leaf type:

Origin plantation or growing region:

Elevation grown:

Ethical notes: Environmental notes:

Number of infusions:

Intensity: Light ---------- Full Bodied

Colour:

Aroma:

Tasting notes:

Other notes on this tea:

Tea name:

Tea Date: Current location:

Brand/Supplier:

Leaf type:

Origin plantation or growing region:

Elevation grown:

Ethical notes: Environmental notes:

Number of infusions:

Intensity: Light ---------- Full Bodied

Colour:

Aroma:

Tasting notes:

Other notes on this tea:

Tea name:

Tea Date: Current location:

Brand/Supplier:

Leaf type:

Origin plantation or growing region:

Elevation grown:

Ethical notes: Environmental notes:

Number of infusions:

Intensity: Light ---------- Full Bodied

Colour:

Aroma:

Tasting notes:

Other notes on this tea:

Tea name:

Tea Date: Current location:

Brand/Supplier:

Leaf type:

Origin plantation or growing region:

Elevation grown:

Ethical notes: Environmental notes:

Number of infusions:

Intensity: Light ---------- Full Bodied

Colour:

Aroma:

Tasting notes:

Other notes on this tea:

Tea name:

Tea Date: Current location:

Brand/Supplier:

Leaf type:

Origin plantation or growing region:

Elevation grown:

Ethical notes: Environmental notes:

Number of infusions:

Intensity: Light ---------- Full Bodied

Colour:

Aroma:

Tasting notes:

Other notes on this tea:

Tea name:

Tea Date: Current location:

Brand/Supplier:

Leaf type:

Origin plantation or growing region:

Elevation grown:

Ethical notes: Environmental notes:

Number of infusions:

Intensity: Light ---------- Full Bodied

Colour:

Aroma:

Tasting notes:

Other notes on this tea:

Tea name:

Tea Date: Current location:

Brand/Supplier:

Leaf type:

Origin plantation or growing region:

Elevation grown:

Ethical notes: Environmental notes:

Number of infusions:

Intensity: Light ---------- Full Bodied

Colour:

Aroma:

Tasting notes:

Other notes on this tea:

Tea name:

Tea Date: Current location:

Brand/Supplier:

Leaf type:

Origin plantation or growing region:

Elevation grown:

Ethical notes: Environmental notes:

Number of infusions:

Intensity: Light ---------- Full Bodied

Colour:

Aroma:

Tasting notes:

Other notes on this tea:

Tea name:

Tea Date: Current location:

Brand/Supplier:

Leaf type:

Origin plantation or growing region:

Elevation grown:

Ethical notes: Environmental notes:

Number of infusions:

Intensity: Light ---------- Full Bodied

Colour:

Aroma:

Tasting notes:

Other notes on this tea:

Tea name:

Tea Date: Current location:

Brand/Supplier:

Leaf type:

Origin plantation or growing region:

Elevation grown:

Ethical notes: Environmental notes:

Number of infusions:

Intensity: Light ---------- Full Bodied

Colour:

Aroma:

Tasting notes:

Other notes on this tea:

Tea name:

Tea Date: Current location:

Brand/Supplier:

Leaf type:

Origin plantation or growing region:

Elevation grown:

Ethical notes: Environmental notes:

Number of infusions:

Intensity: Light ---------- Full Bodied

Colour:

Aroma:

Tasting notes:

Other notes on this tea:

Tea name:

Tea Date: Current location:

Brand/Supplier:

Leaf type:

Origin plantation or growing region:

Elevation grown:

Ethical notes: Environmental notes:

Number of infusions:

Intensity: Light ---------- Full Bodied

Colour:

Aroma:

Tasting notes:

Other notes on this tea:

Tea name:

Tea Date: Current location:

Brand/Supplier:

Leaf type:

Origin plantation or growing region:

Elevation grown:

Ethical notes: Environmental notes:

Number of infusions:

Intensity: Light ---------- Full Bodied

Colour:

Aroma:

Tasting notes:

Other notes on this tea:

Tea name:

Tea Date: Current location:

Brand/Supplier:

Leaf type:

Origin plantation or growing region:

Elevation grown:

Ethical notes: Environmental notes:

Number of infusions:

Intensity: Light ---------- Full Bodied

Colour:

Aroma:

Tasting notes:

Other notes on this tea:

Tea name:

Tea Date: Current location:

Brand/Supplier:

Leaf type:

Origin plantation or growing region:

Elevation grown:

Ethical notes: Environmental notes:

Number of infusions:

Intensity: Light ---------- Full Bodied

Colour:

Aroma:

Tasting notes:

Other notes on this tea:

Tea name:

Tea Date: Current location:

Brand/Supplier:

Leaf type:

Origin plantation or growing region:

Elevation grown:

Ethical notes: Environmental notes:

Number of infusions:

Intensity: Light ---------- Full Bodied

Colour:

Aroma:

Tasting notes:

Other notes on this tea:

Tea name:

Tea Date: Current location:

Brand/Supplier:

Leaf type:

Origin plantation or growing region:

Elevation grown:

Ethical notes: Environmental notes:

Number of infusions:

Intensity: Light ---------- Full Bodied

Colour:

Aroma:

Tasting notes:

Other notes on this tea:

Tea name:

Tea Date: Current location:

Brand/Supplier:

Leaf type:

Origin plantation or growing region:

Elevation grown:

Ethical notes: Environmental notes:

Number of infusions:

Intensity: Light ---------- Full Bodied

Colour:

Aroma:

Tasting notes:

Other notes on this tea:

Tea name:

Tea Date: Current location:

Brand/Supplier:

Leaf type:

Origin plantation or growing region:

Elevation grown:

Ethical notes: Environmental notes:

Number of infusions:

Intensity: Light ---------- Full Bodied

Colour:

Aroma:

Tasting notes:

Other notes on this tea:

Tea name:

Tea Date: Current location:

Brand/Supplier:

Leaf type:

Origin plantation or growing region:

Elevation grown:

Ethical notes: Environmental notes:

Number of infusions:

Intensity: Light ---------- Full Bodied

Colour:

Aroma:

Tasting notes:

Other notes on this tea:

Tea name:

Tea Date: Current location:

Brand/Supplier:

Leaf type:

Origin plantation or growing region:

Elevation grown:

Ethical notes: Environmental notes:

Number of infusions:

Intensity: Light ---------- Full Bodied

Colour:

Aroma:

Tasting notes:

Other notes on this tea:

Tea name:

Tea Date: Current location:

Brand/Supplier:

Leaf type:

Origin plantation or growing region:

Elevation grown:

Ethical notes: Environmental notes:

Number of infusions:

Intensity: Light ---------- Full Bodied

Colour:

Aroma:

Tasting notes:

Other notes on this tea:

Tea name:

Tea Date: Current location:

Brand/Supplier:

Leaf type:

Origin plantation or growing region:

Elevation grown:

Ethical notes: Environmental notes:

Number of infusions:

Intensity: Light ---------- Full Bodied

Colour:

Aroma:

Tasting notes:

Other notes on this tea:

Tea name:

Tea Date: Current location:

Brand/Supplier:

Leaf type:

Origin plantation or growing region:

Elevation grown:

Ethical notes: Environmental notes:

Number of infusions:

Intensity: Light ---------- Full Bodied

Colour:

Aroma:

Tasting notes:

Other notes on this tea:

Tea name:

Tea Date: Current location:

Brand/Supplier:

Leaf type:

Origin plantation or growing region:

Elevation grown:

Ethical notes: Environmental notes:

Number of infusions:

Intensity: Light ---------- Full Bodied

Colour:

Aroma:

Tasting notes:

Other notes on this tea:

Tea name:

Tea Date: Current location:

Brand/Supplier:

Leaf type:

Origin plantation or growing region:

Elevation grown:

Ethical notes: Environmental notes:

Number of infusions:

Intensity: Light ---------- Full Bodied

Colour:

Aroma:

Tasting notes:

Other notes on this tea:

Tea name:

Tea Date: Current location:

Brand/Supplier:

Leaf type:

Origin plantation or growing region:

Elevation grown:

Ethical notes: Environmental notes:

Number of infusions:

Intensity: Light ---------- Full Bodied

Colour:

Aroma:

Tasting notes:

Other notes on this tea:

Tea name:

Tea Date: Current location:

Brand/Supplier:

Leaf type:

Origin plantation or growing region:

Elevation grown:

Ethical notes: Environmental notes:

Number of infusions:

Intensity: Light ---------- Full Bodied

Colour:

Aroma:

Tasting notes:

Other notes on this tea:

Tea name:

Tea Date: Current location:

Brand/Supplier:

Leaf type:

Origin plantation or growing region:

Elevation grown:

Ethical notes: Environmental notes:

Number of infusions:

Intensity: Light ---------- Full Bodied

Colour:

Aroma:

Tasting notes:

Other notes on this tea:

Keeping in touch

You can share your tea adventures with us by following and tagging us on the following social media links. Please do say hello, we would to hear from you!

Twitter: @tea_lama
Instagram: @thetealama
Facebook Page: Art and Tea

You can visit our website to learn more about, tea, the universe and Buddhism, and also shop at our ethical tea shop to support our work. We regularly organise events across the world and monthly events within the UK, please do come along!

www.chadao.co.uk

ABOUT THE AUTHOR

In my 39 years in this life, I've never grown up. I've never quite understood how I got here, even after meeting myself three times. But life so far has been immense amounts of drinking tea and attempting to understand how to change the world to help others.

I'm never sure what to write when it comes to myself, and I most certainly don't do 'sales pitch' style promotion. I trained as an artist when I was a teenager, eventually becoming a graphic and product designer, that went well, I went on to start and run three highly successful business and then one total and utter failure, which perhaps had the most positive impact on everyone I know.

I still paint watercolours, still learn Buddhist Philosophy, still go off on adventures. Most importantly, more than ever I teach. Not mathematics or science, English or useful things, I hope I teach how to inspire, how to help others become better people, and in doing so learn from them to better oneself.

As a non-monastic I live a simple life, on a very small wooden sailboat, with a cat named Banjo and a lifelong companion dog called Teacup (Who is the more famous of our Trio). Sometimes I spend time at a monastery, teaching, learning, laughing, all to brief moments before the call to the outside world's community pulls me back.

Scouting is a huge part of my life, at every opportunity I have been impressed by the community of Scouts worldwide and locally. The privilege of sharing the adventures of scouting teenagers on their own life paths is something I am always thankful for.

I hope you forgive this simple "About the Author" page, without it's glowing past glories, but this I trust is more intimate, hopefully showing you simply, who I am.

Ven. Cha Lama Tenzin Yun Tony Malone
Onboard Sailing Bawley GladTimes, 2018, London.

Tiger Hill, Darjeeling, Where my own adventures in tea started a long time ago.